The British Medical Association

DK

FAMILY DOCTOR GUIDE *to*

BACK PAIN

PROFESSOR MALCOLM JAYSON

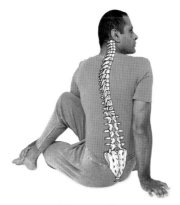

MEDICAL EDITOR
DR. TONY SMITH

DORLING KINDERSLEY
LONDON • NEW YORK • SYDNEY • MOSCOW
www.dk.com

IMPORTANT

This book is not designed as a substitute for personal medical advice but as a supplement to that advice for the patient who wishes to understand more about his/her condition.

Before taking any form of treatment **YOU SHOULD ALWAYS CONSULT YOUR MEDICAL PRACTITIONER.**

In particular (without limit) you should note that advances in medical science occur rapidly and some of the information contained in this book about drugs and treatment may very soon be out of date.

PLEASE NOTE

The author regrets that he cannot enter into any correspondence with readers.

A DORLING KINDERSLEY BOOK
www.dk.com

Senior Editor Mary Lindsay
Senior Designer Sarah Hall
Production Assistant Elizabeth Cherry

Managing Editor Stephanie Jackson
Managing Art Editor Nigel Duffield

Produced for Dorling Kindersley Limited by
Design Revolution, Queens Park Villa,
30 West Drive, Brighton, East Sussex BN2 2GE
Editorial Director Ian Whitelaw
Art Director Fiona Roberts
Editor Julie Whitaker
Designer Vanessa Good

Published in Great Britain in 1999 by
Dorling Kindersley Limited,
9 Henrietta Street, London WC2E 8PS

2 4 6 8 10 9 7 5 3 1

A CIP catalogue record for this book is available from the British Library

ISBN 07513 0670 3

Reproduced by Colourscan, Singapore
Printed in Hong Kong by Wing King Tong

00003415

Medical Association

Contents

Introduction

Backache is not an illness in itself, but a symptom. Its development means something has gone wrong somewhere, although it may not always be clear exactly what.

Most of us suffer from backache at some time or other. Usually it is an unpleasant and awkward, but not desperately serious, problem caused by some kind of mechanical stress or damage within the back, which gets better fairly quickly. Poor posture, excessive stresses, and wear and tear problems may be at least partly responsible.

You should not be surprised that backache is so common when you realise that your spine is composed of many different structures, including bones, discs, ligaments, tendons, nerves, blood vessels and other tissues, all of which can be affected by mechanical damage resulting in backache.

In most cases the precise cause of the problem is not important. Backache is a symptom that will clear up and the purpose of treatment is to relieve pain and to make sure that you recover as soon as possible. Occasionally there may be a more severe underlying cause and detailed investigations are required to decide the right approach to treatment. Understanding how the back works will help us to protect our spines and recover more rapidly from episodes of backache.

WHO GETS BACKACHE?
Backache is a common complaint that affects almost everyone at some time in their lives, but it is rarely serious.

This book aims to show you how the back works, what goes wrong, why back problems arise, how they are treated and to give some indication of when further investigations and specialised help are necessary.

A GROWING PROBLEM

Backache is remarkably common. At any one time some 30–40 per cent of the population have backache and between 80 and 90 per cent experience it at some time in their lives. It affects both sexes and all ages, from children to elderly people, but is most prevalent in the middle years.

Backache is one of the most common reasons why people have to take time off work, especially in heavy manual industries. At particular risk are workers in the building industry and nurses, as in both cases they often have to undertake heavy lifts in awkward postures.

It is often hard to separate cause and effect: in other words, do the stresses in the job cause the backache, or is the person unable to do heavy work because they already have a bad back? In many cases, back pain follows some injury or a sudden twist. Much time is now spent training workers to avoid subjecting their backs to excessive stresses.

The amount of working time lost due to back problems has increased enormously in recent years. It is now running at some 100,000,000 working days per year in England and Wales, two or three times more than 20 years ago. In fact, this dramatic rise does not mean that more people are being injured at work. Rather, it reflects the more concerned approach taken by both workers and employers to the effects of back pain.

HEAVY WORK
Lifting a heavy weight need not strain the back if the right technique is used. Always bend your hips and knees rather than your back.

Common Back Complaints

Back pain varies widely from one person to another, depending on lifestyle and occupation, but the following are common complaints:

- 'I work in a factory assembling components. By the end of the day I have a terrible aching pain low down in my back, and I really don't know how much longer I can stand it.'
- 'I am not too bad during the day, but I wake up in the morning with a lot of pain and stiffness in my back and have to get up and move around before it eases.'
- 'I was just bending over to pick up a book from the floor when felt a sudden severe pain in the bottom of my back, and I couldn't straighten up.'
- 'While I was working in the garden, I got a twinge of pain in my lower back. Over the next few hours the pain spread into my bottom and down the back of my leg. It really hurt, and I had to go to bed.'

BACKACHE AND WORK
Standing in an awkward position for prolonged periods at work can exacerbate a back problem, resulting in considerable pain by the end of the day.

The result is a dramatic escalation in the costs of back pain to our society. The total cost is now calculated as being nearly £6,000,000,000 per year for the medical treatment provided, the benefits received, and loss of production – a phenomenal sum.

The increase in the numbers of people disabled by back problems has led to a complete rethink of our approach to back pain and how it is

9

treated. In this book I will provide the most up-to-date views based on the latest research on the treatment of back pain, and explain how we are attempting to reduce the frequency and severity of this problem.

KEY POINTS

- Backache is a symptom, not a disease.
- Acute episodes of back pain, although unpleasant, usually get better quickly.
- Backache affects 80–90 per cent of the population at some time in their lives.

How the spine works

The spine or back bone is known medically as the vertebral column. Its role is to support the whole body, be capable of bending and twisting in all directions, and at the same time protect the vital structures, such as nerves, that run through it. What's more, it has to last a lifetime.

THE FLEXIBLE BODY
The spine can bend and twist because there are flexible discs allowing mobility between the vertebrae.

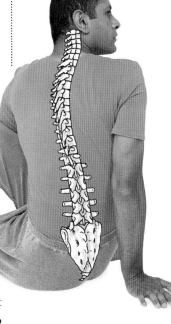

No engineering structure comes anywhere near meeting the exacting specifications of the spine, and it is hardly surprising that problems can arise from time to time.

THE VERTEBRAL COLUMN

The human spine consists of a column of bony blocks known as vertebrae, which sit one on top of another to form the vertebral column. There are seven cervical vertebrae in the neck, twelve dorsal or thoracic vertebrae in the upper and middle back and five lumbar vertebrae in the lower part of the spine. The fifth lumbar vertebra, known as L5, sits on the sacrum which in turn is connected to the coccyx – the tail bone. The sacrum consists of several vertebrae that have joined together. The sacrum is joined at its edges to

The Spine – Back View

Seen from the back, the spine is a vertical column of vertebrae, attached to the pelvis at the bottom, and supporting the skull at the top. The cervical vertebrae in the neck allow the skull to rotate and to tilt in all directions.

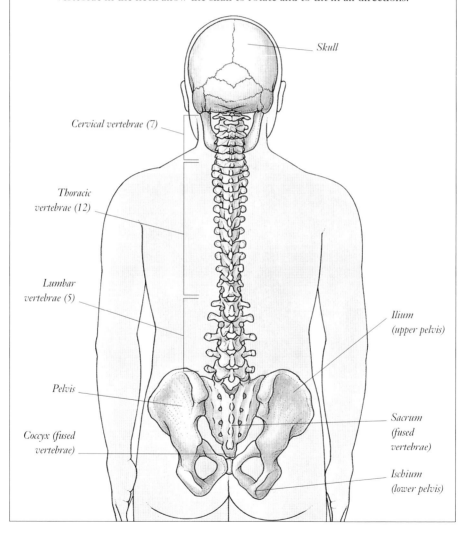

Skull

Cervical vertebrae (7)

Thoracic vertebrae (12)

Lumbar vertebrae (5)

Ilium (upper pelvis)

Pelvis

Sacrum (fused vertebrae)

Coccyx (fused vertebrae)

Ischium (lower pelvis)

The Spine – Side View

Seen from the side, the spine has a pronounced curve. The lumbar vertebrae, in the lower back, have long bony extensions to which strong muscles are attached. The sacrum and coccyx at the bottom of the spine consist of several fused vertebrae.

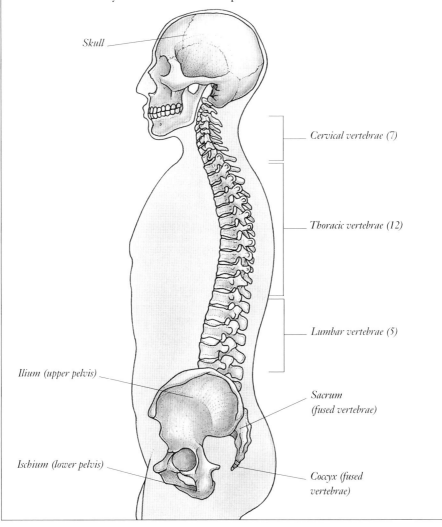

Skull

Cervical vertebrae (7)

Thoracic vertebrae (12)

Lumbar vertebrae (5)

Ilium (upper pelvis)

Sacrum
(fused vertebrae)

Ischium (lower pelvis)

Coccyx (fused
vertebrae)

the pelvis – the ring of bone that carries the trunk and which in turn is supported by the hips.

INTERVERTEBRAL DISCS

The spine is able to bend and twist because there are flexible cushions or discs between the vertebrae. Each disc is a flat structure with a jelly-like centre called the nucleus and an extremely strong outer skin called the annulus.

The Structure of the Spine

The vertebrae are separated from one another by flexible intervertebral discs. Nerves leave the spinal cord through small bony openings between the vertebrae.

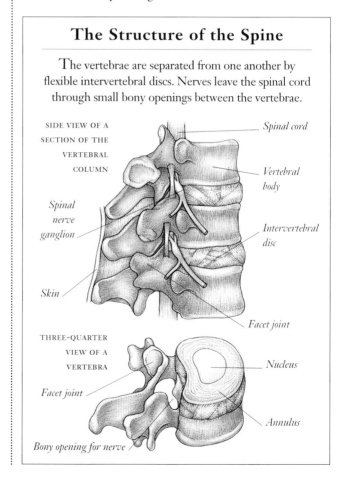

SIDE VIEW OF A SECTION OF THE VERTEBRAL COLUMN

Spinal cord

Vertebral body

Spinal nerve ganglion

Intervertebral disc

Skin

Facet joint

THREE-QUARTER VIEW OF A VERTEBRA

Nucleus

Facet joint

Annulus

Bony opening for nerve

14

The Nerve Network

The spinal cord is the main nerve 'cable', connecting the nerves of the limbs and torso to the brain. The bony vertebral column surrounds and protects the spinal cord.

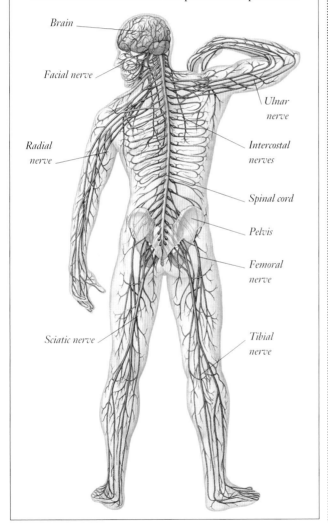

Brain

Facial nerve

Ulnar nerve

Radial nerve

Intercostal nerves

Spinal cord

Pelvis

Femoral nerve

Sciatic nerve

Tibial nerve

15

FACET JOINTS

The vertebrae are also joined to each other by pairs of small joints which lie at the back of the spine, one on either side. They can be affected by strain or by wear and tear and may develop bony swellings causing pressure on nerves.

NERVE NETWORK

The nervous system in some ways resembles a telephone network carrying messages from your brain to various parts of your body and back again (see p.15). Messages that pass down nerves make muscles contract and so control movements such as walking. Messages travelling up nerves carry sensations that eventually reach your brain so you experience sensations such as touch and pain.

SPINAL CORD

A 'cable' of nervous tissue, known as the spinal cord, extends from the brain down the spine inside the canal formed by the vertebrae. The nerve roots divide off from the spinal cord, run for short distances within the canal itself and then emerge in pairs, one on each side, from the sides of the vertebral column to supply the trunk, the arms, and the legs.

BACK INJURIES

The fact that the spinal cord carries messages to and from the body means that if it is damaged, the 'connection' may be affected, and this can lead to the loss or alteration of sensation, development of pain, and weakness of movements. This is what happens when people become paralysed after a serious accident. The number of limbs paralysed, i.e. whether they can move their arms and not their legs, or whether all four limbs are paralysed, depends on where the spinal cord has been damaged. If the injury is in the neck, paralysis and loss of sensation can affect both the arms and the legs.

However, if the injury is in the thoracic or lumbar segments – below the arm level – then only leg muscles are affected. In most back problems the nerves are damaged, but not the spinal cord.

Pain can develop in the back itself as a result of direct injuries to the ligaments, tendons, joints and other structures in and around the vertebral column, but because the same nerves that supply these tissues also supply the legs, patients may experience the pain as if it is arising from the legs.

In addition, there may be pressure directly on the nerves, also producing pain, alteration in the sense of feeling, and weakness in the legs.

It is clear that the back is a very complicated structure. When there has been some injury, back pain may arise for several different reasons. Very careful analysis would be necessary to determine what has happened in any individual. Fortunately, most acute episodes of back pain get better without the need for specific forms of intervention.

As a result, very detailed tests to determine the particular injuries causing problems are generally not required. However, when symptoms are more serious and prolonged it becomes important to determine exactly what is going wrong. Very careful examination and diagnostic tests, including some of the newer forms of imaging, may then become necessary.

KEY POINTS

- The vertebral column consists of vertebrae joined by discs and facet joints. The disc has a jelly-like central nucleus and an extremely strong outer skin, the annulus.
- Back pain may arise from damage to a wide variety of structures.
- Back pain is transmitted by the nerves. The ways that these are stimulated are complex and depend upon the particular tissue or type of nerve that has been affected.
- As most acute episodes of back pain get better quickly, there is usually no need for very detailed tests to determine the precise cause.

Some common back problems

Now we know the make-up of the spine, it is easier to understand where and why problems can arise.

NON-SPECIFIC BACK PAIN

Many people who have trouble with their backs experience brief episodes of pain from which they make a full recovery. No firm diagnosis is made, and so their back pain is called non-specific. Detailed investigations are not necessary and often it is not possible to identify the particular underlying cause. Sometimes the person has tender areas over the spine or between the sacrum and the iliac bone of the pelvis. The pain may be caused by strains of ligaments, tendons or other soft tissues.

Although the cause is usually uncertain, terms such as lumbosacral strain and sacroiliac strain are often used, implying that your doctor has actually made a diagnosis. The term 'non-specific back pain' is preferable, as it does not suggest that we know the cause of your particular problem. Further investigation to pinpoint the cause is only necessary if the back pain fails to settle.

BRIEF EPISODES OF PAIN
Most back pain of sudden onset, such as that experienced when getting up from a sitting position, has no identifiable cause.

19

SLIPPED DISCS

Most people have heard of a 'slipped disc' but it is a rather inaccurate name because discs cannot actually slip. They can wear, split or burst. What happens is that, after some stress on the spine – often involving bending, twisting or lifting – the disc bursts or prolapses and the jelly-like central nucleus is squeezed out through a split in the outer annulus.

Effects of a Prolapsed Vertebral Disc

Every intervertebral disc has a fibrous outer layer, or annulus, surrounding the jelly-like nucleus. Under stress, its annulus can rupture, forcing out the nucleus, which can then press on the nerve root, as this spinal cross-section shows.

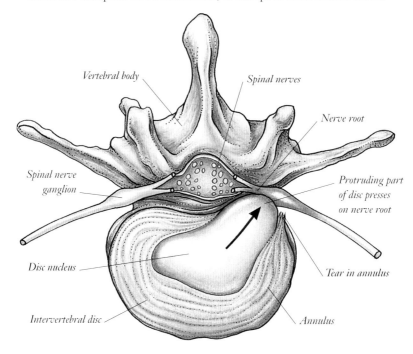

Vertebral body

Spinal nerves

Nerve root

Spinal nerve ganglion

Protruding part of disc presses on nerve root

Disc nucleus

Tear in annulus

Intervertebral disc

Annulus

We now believe that most discs that prolapse in this way previously had some wear and tear changes and that the stress on the spine then triggered the problem. In other words, the disc was already abnormal and would have burst sooner or later anyway. The particular stress probably just acted as the 'final straw'.

The jelly-like material, having been squeezed out, presses on the nerve running next to the disc, causing severe pain in the back that spreads down the leg and sometimes as far as the foot. You may feel numbness and tingling, particularly in your lower leg and foot. Some of your muscles may become weak and the ankle jerk reflex, tested by tapping your Achilles tendon with a tendon hammer, may be lost.

The site of these changes helps the doctor to identify exactly which nerve has been damaged.

The pain caused by a burst disc can be very severe. Usually the symptoms will slowly get better and eventually disappear completely. However, once the disc has burst, it is permanently weak and there is always the risk of a further bout of back pain.

SCIATICA

As the greatest weight and bending forces are experienced in the lower part of the lumbar spine, the nerves most often damaged are the fifth lumbar nerve root (which leaves the spine between the fourth and fifth lumbar vertebrae) and the first sacral root (which leaves the spine between the fifth lumbar vertebra and the first part of the sacrum). These two nerves join with others to form the sciatic nerve, which runs down the back of the leg to the foot. Pain arising because of damage to this nerve is known as sciatica.

Sciatic Nerves

The sciatic nerves are the largest nerves in the body.
They run from the lumbar and sacral regions of the
spine, and then down the backs of the legs.

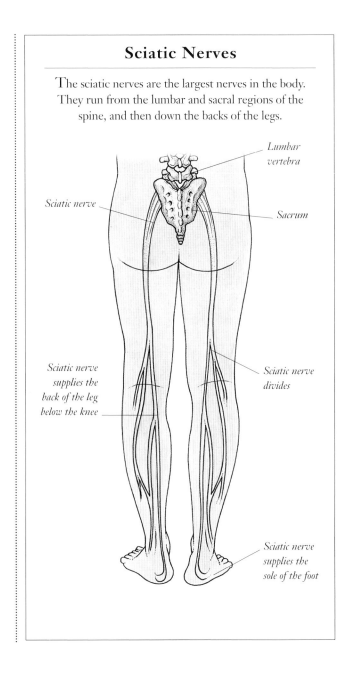

Lumbar vertebra

Sciatic nerve

Sacrum

Sciatic nerve supplies the back of the leg below the knee

Sciatic nerve divides

Sciatic nerve supplies the sole of the foot

LUMBAR SPONDYLOSIS

Spondylosis, or wear and tear of the spine, is very common. Indeed, these changes start at the age of about 25 and are present in almost all of us by the time we are middle-aged. This is one of the main reasons why athletes are at the peak of their performance in their early twenties.

The lower back bears the weight of your whole body, as well as anything that you're carrying, and does most of the bending and twisting. This is why wear and tear

How Wear and Tear Affects the Spine

Wear and tear in the lower part of the back (known as lumbar spondylosis) is extremely common. This part of the spine bears the weight of the whole body, as well as doing most of the bending and twisting, and is therefore easily damaged.

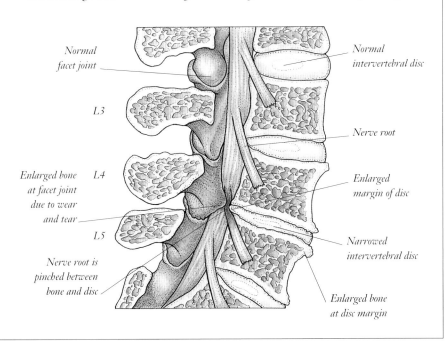

Normal facet joint

Normal intervertebral disc

L3

Nerve root

Enlarged bone at facet joint due to wear and tear

L4

Enlarged margin of disc

L5

Narrowed intervertebral disc

Nerve root is pinched between bone and disc

Enlarged bone at disc margin

changes of the spine are most common in the lumbar region, and are called lumbar spondylosis.

Lumbar spondylosis is most likely to occur at the lower levels, particularly between the fourth and fifth lumbar vertebrae (L4/L5) and the fifth lumbar vertebra and the first segment of the sacrum (L5/S1), and leads to sciatica (see p.21). It affects both the discs and the facet joints. Some material is lost from the disc and from the cartilage or gristle lining the facet joints. The bone at the margins of the discs and facet joints enlarges, making movement more limited and so stiffening the spine. It may press on nerves, ligaments and other structures causing pain.

However, this is not as depressing as it sounds. The fact that you have these wear and tear changes does not mean that you are bound to get backache. Many people have quite severe wear and tear changes with few or no problems, whereas others with relatively minor changes suffer incapacitating bouts of pain. It follows that wear and tear changes of this sort are generally of only minor significance.

PEAK PERFORMANCE
An athlete reaches his peak at the age of about 25, after which general wear and tear on the joints of the spine starts to affect performance.

LUMBAGO

One of the most common back problems is recurrent spells of acute pain that may spread to the buttocks or to one or other thigh. While the attack lasts, your back may also feel stiff and tender. When the symptoms are very severe the condition is called lumbago. The pain can last for a day or two or up to a couple of weeks each time. Sometimes it then disappears completely or it may persist or recur. The symptoms are made worse by poor posture and heavy lifting.

X-rays frequently show the presence of lumbar spondylosis, but surveys have revealed that these changes are often found in people who don't have any symptoms. It is therefore difficult to assess the part they have played in causing pain. As a result, the term 'non-specific back pain' is often used to describe lumbago.

NERVE PROBLEMS

Nerves easily get squashed, within the vertebral canal and as they emerge from the sides of the vertebral column, by damaged discs, facet joints or vertebrae. When a nerve is squashed its ability to pass messages is affected. When this happens, you may experience pain or a sensation of numbness or tingling in the area supplied by the nerve, and the muscles that it controls in your leg or foot may become weak. The spinal cord transmits these sensations to the brain – it is a bit like interference on a telephone wire, producing unpleasant noises and poor quality sound. In fact, current research indicates that it is a great deal more complicated than that.

Changes within the spinal cord itself can affect the pain message. This may explain why some patients continue to experience widespread and prolonged symptoms when the original nerve damage has healed and there is little evidence of much wrong with the back.

COCCYDYNIA

This is the name given to pain at the tail end of the spine, or the coccyx. Usually no cause for the pain is found. A soft cushion ring may be used to make sitting more comfortable, but the condition usually settles by itself with time.

RELIEVING THE PRESSURE
A soft ring-shaped cushion will make sitting more comfortable if you are suffering from an injury to the coccyx.

25

NECK PROBLEMS

This section will deal only briefly with common neck disorders. The neck shares the same basic structure as the rest of the spine, and is therefore also prone to disc problems and wear and tear changes.

While pain in the lower back commonly shoots down the legs, neck pain may involve the shoulders and arms. For uncomplicated neck problems, treatment with rest, painkillers and perhaps physiotherapy usually suffices. A padded neck collar is helpful to ensure that the neck is properly supported and rested.

ACUTE STIFF NECK SYNDROME

Many people have had the experience of waking up with a stiff and painful neck, often it seems for no particular reason. Movement may only be possible in one direction, and the muscles of the lower neck may be tender. There are no other problems with the rest of the back or the arms or legs. The pain is associated with muscle spasm and will settle with a collar and painkillers in three to four days. Occasionally very gentle neck traction may help.

WHIPLASH

This is common after a car accident, when the sudden impact gives no time for muscles to brace, and the head moves like a pendulum on the neck. In the simplest cases only ligaments in the neck are sprained, and the pain and stiffness that result are caused by the neck muscles going into spasm as a protective mechanism. If there are no other problems, a soft collar, pain relief, and occasionally physiotherapy are all that are needed. For most patients early return to normal activity gives the best results. In

How Whiplash Occurs

Whiplash injury commonly results from a front impact car accident. The neck is forced suddenly forwards and then backwards, spraining the ligaments.

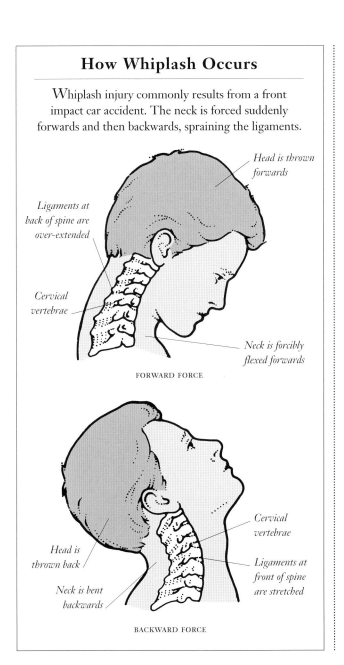

Head is thrown forwards

Ligaments at back of spine are over-extended

Cervical vertebrae

Neck is forcibly flexed forwards

FORWARD FORCE

Cervical vertebrae

Ligaments at front of spine are stretched

Head is thrown back

Neck is bent backwards

BACKWARD FORCE

27

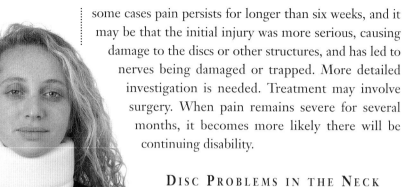

some cases pain persists for longer than six weeks, and it may be that the initial injury was more serious, causing damage to the discs or other structures, and has led to nerves being damaged or trapped. More detailed investigation is needed. Treatment may involve surgery. When pain remains severe for several months, it becomes more likely there will be continuing disability.

DISC PROBLEMS IN THE NECK

Discs can also prolapse in the neck, although this is less common than in the lower back. The neck is extremely stiff, and pain may shoot down one arm. Strength, sensation and reflexes in the arm

USING A NECK COLLAR
After a whiplash injury, a neck collar provides support and restricts excessive movement until muscle spasm has settled.

may be lost. In the majority of cases, the pain will settle with rest, pain relief, traction if necessary, and a period of gentle activation with a collar. Physiotherapy to strengthen the neck muscles is also useful.

WEAR AND TEAR PROBLEMS

These changes are extremely common in the neck, and are known as cervical spondylosis. They may cause no problems at all, or lead to neck pain with headache and/or arm pain. Neck movements are reduced, and some patients have a tender spot in the trapezius muscle, which lies between the neck and the shoulders. Again, the arms may become weak and lose their reflexes. There may be tingling or pins and needles in the arms. In the most serious cases, the distorted bone and ligaments can press on the spinal cord, affecting control of the arms and legs, or on an artery in the region, called the vertebral artery, leading to dizziness, a buzzing in the ear and pain behind the eyes.

Many people who have cervical spondylosis also have low back pain. The principles of treatment are the same: use a collar, physiotherapy, anti-inflammatory drugs, pain relief and early mobilisation. Surgery may be necessary for a small proportion of patients.

KEY POINTS

- Discs do not slip, but they can burst.
- Sciatica is caused by damage to either of the two nerves that join to form the sciatic nerve running down the lower limb.
- Wear and tear or spondylosis of the spine is very common as you get older, but does not inevitably lead to back pain.
- Neck problems have many similarities to back pain.

Treating back pain – the first steps

SIMPLE BACK PAIN
Some back pain, for example the discomfort experienced after a long drive, may disappear within a few minutes on stretching your back and moving about.

Most of us get sudden episodes of pain in the back from time to time, usually lasting only a day or so. Apart from being careful, you do not need to do anything about it and it is soon forgotten. Some people, however, may develop more severe attacks of pain which limit their activity and their ability to work.

Despite all our modern technology, in many cases we are not able to determine the exact source of our back pain. It could well be the result of some damage to the ligaments, muscles or other soft tissues, but often your doctor may be unable to determine the precise cause. The good news, however, is that generally it does not matter, as most of these acute attacks of back pain will get better without treatment.

The most common problem is simple backache, in which the pain is confined to the back or may spread down into the buttock or upper thigh. Sometimes it may extend right down the leg affecting the sciatic nerve, giving rise to sciatica. Pressure on this nerve may come from a damaged disc or other structures, causing pain and sometimes numbness and tingling running down your leg. Sciatica suggests that there has been some nerve damage and that recovery is likely to be slow.

Occasionally, a person may develop more severe symptoms of a back problem, which mean that they need to be seen quickly by a specialist. This will be necessary for any person who experiences any problems controlling the bladder or bowel, any numbness in the groin or rectal area, or severe leg weakness, as it could be a sign of more severe nerve damage.

ASSESSING THE PROBLEM

Usually, when you have an acute back problem, the person treating you will ask for details about how and when the pain started and what has happened since, and give you a physical examination. Questions that you may be asked include:

- Is the pain confined to one area only or is it more generalised?
- Does the pain shoot or spread to another part of the body, for example, to the leg?
- How did the pain come on – suddenly or gradually? If gradually, over what period of time?
- Was the onset associated with any activity?
- Does anything make the pain worse?
- What is the pain like first thing in the morning?
- Are you otherwise well? Have you lost weight/got a cough/other problems?

VISITING A SPECIALIST
If your back pain is severe, you will be referred to a specialist for assessment.

31

A pain that started on lifting a heavy object, that is sharp and limited to a small area, and that is relieved with rest is likely to be uncomplicated, and the pain should get better rapidly. However, if the pain began gradually over many months, does not seem to be linked with movement, and is becoming more severe, and if there are other problems, such as weight loss, then the cause may be more serious, and special investigations may be necessary.

You may be sent for an X-ray, but usually this is not necessary. Although it may well show that you have some wear and tear changes, these features are common in

A Specialist Back Examination

If your back pain does not clear up of its own accord, you may be sent to a specialist for further examination. The specialist may carry out some or all of the following procedures:

- Look for signs of curvature, and observe the way that it bends and how you walk.
- Feel your back for tender spots or areas.
- Perform the straight-leg raising test. The doctor lifts each leg straight up, while you are lying flat on your back. If there is a problem with the sciatic nerve, this will bring on the pain.
- Perform the femoral stretch test. The doctor places you lying down on your front, then slowly bends each knee in turn. If there is a problem with another nerve, called the femoral nerve, this will bring on the pain.
- Look for loss of sensation or weakness in the legs.
- Check your reflexes.

people without backache and so don't have much influence on the choice of treatment. Each X-ray exposes you to radiation, which is why they should be reserved for people with severe back pain that has not responded to simple treatment and for those who have more complicated back problems.

You are unlikely to need more detailed types of imaging, such as magnetic resonance imaging (MRI) or computed tomography (CT) scans (see p57).

HOW IS IT TREATED?

For most people with acute back pain only very simple treatment is needed:

● Take simple pain-relieving tablets such as paracetamol or ibuprofen. These tablets have few side effects and are usually all you will need. You can ask your doctor for stronger painkillers, which are available on prescription, if you feel that you need them.

● A short period of bedrest is helpful, but too much can actually aggravate the problems. If you're in severe pain, you should rest lying flat in bed for a couple of days. After that, you can start to move around again, taking care to protect your back, but aiming to return towards normal physical activity.

● A cold pack – such as a bag of ice or frozen peas – against your back may help to relieve the pain. Alternatively, you can try heat in the form of a heating pad or a hot shower. However, neither is likely to make any long-term difference.

For most people, simple remedies such as these are enough and the pain will usually clear within a few days or a couple of weeks. You should aim to get back to normal physical activity as soon as possible. It is important that you take note of the advice in the chapter on how to protect your back so as to reduce your chances of having another attack in the future (see Protecting your back, pp.37–44).

You may, however, be one of the unlucky ones whose pain does not disappear completely. If you still have a problem after about four to six weeks, you need to see a therapist. This might be:

- A doctor with special expertise in the appropriate treatment techniques;
- A physiotherapist;
- An osteopath;
- A chiropractor.

BACK THERAPY
Trained therapists can assess back conditions and ease pain by massage and exercise.

Physiotherapy is the more traditional form of physical therapy, and it usually involves the use of heat, gentle massage and exercise to help someone regain movement, strength and suppleness. Many physiotherapists are also trained in manipulation.

Both osteopathy and chiropractic treatments tend to concentrate on joint manipulation. In general, a chiropractor is likely to use quick, gentle, specific thrusts, whereas an osteopath tends to use slower, more general movements. All therapists will give advice on the care and protection of the back. In practice, however, it is doubtful whether there is much to choose between these techniques, as in all cases, the principles behind treatment are the same, and include physical activation with exercises of various types and manipulation. The treatment for sciatica (see p.21) also involves pain-relieving tablets, rest and remobilisation, but progress is often a lot slower. Sometimes people with this particular problem have to be referred for surgery to relieve the pressure on the nerve. More information on persistent back pain is given in the next two chapters.

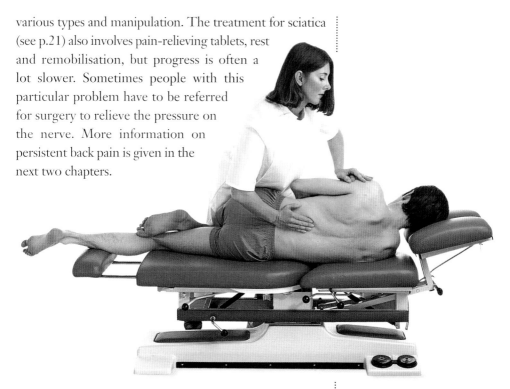

MANIPULATIVE THERAPY
Manipulating the joints of the spine can help to restore mobility.

RECURRENT BACK PAIN

The natural history of most acute back episodes is recovery, commonly in a few days but sometimes taking a week or even a few weeks.

People with a history of back pain are likely to develop further episodes in the future. Sometimes recurrences are the result of an accident or an exceptional load, but for many people acute relapses may be precipitated by quite trivial physical activities. Understanding how the back works and minimising stresses on the spine, together with improvement in physical fitness, will help to prevent further lapses from occurring.

KEY POINTS

- Most acute back pain is simple backache. A small proportion of people have sciatica, and a few have more complicated problems.
- Simple backache usually responds to pain relief, a short period of bed rest if necessary and then early physical activation and return to work.
- If it fails to improve, you may need to see a therapist or a specialist who may undertake further investigations and treatment.

Protecting your back

Some people who start off with an underlying back weakness go through repeated bouts of back pain, often because of a combination of poor posture and excessive stresses on the back.

We now know how different positions and loads affect the back and may lead to back problems, but you can teach yourself how to minimise the stresses you place on your back. These lessons are actually important for all of us, but especially for anyone who is susceptible to back pain.

IMPROVING YOUR POSTURE

How we stand and sit is important and may greatly affect our ability to cope with back pain. Taking care over this will minimise a lot of stresses on your spine. Standing badly can stretch the spinal ligaments and cause aching and stiffness in your back. The following tips will help improve your posture:

• Stand upright with your back straight and your head facing forwards, and avoid slouching.

• When you're working at a bench, check that it is high enough to stand with a good comfortable working posture and, in particular, that you can stand upright.

POOR POSTURE
Standing badly, with a curved spine, will eventually lead to back pain. Always stand upright with your weight balanced evenly on both feet.

- A desk should be of sufficient height and with leg space so you are close enough to sit upright and work comfortably. There should be enough room beneath the work surface so that you can get close to your work without having to bend forwards and also to allow free movement of your legs and feet.

- Keeping still in one position for a long time is an important cause of aching and stiffness.

- When sitting at a desk, ensure that you can sit upright with a support in the small of your back.

THE WORK STATION
Ensure that you can get close to your work without having to bend forwards. It is also important to sit upright when working at a desk. If necessary, use a raised surface, as this man is doing.

EXAMINING YOUR SHOES

Women who get back pain should not wear high heels. They tip the lower part of your body forwards, and you then arch your upper body backwards to compensate, so putting stress on your back. It is better to opt for shoes that do not have hard leather soles; hard soles send shock waves up through your skeleton as your heels strike the ground and often aggravate back problems. Cushioned soles and heels or shock-absorbing insoles can reduce this and often make walking much easier. I recommend trainers, as they are so comfortable and minimise these sudden shock waves.

DRIVING COMFORTABLY

Backache is common in all of us who spend long periods driving. Anyone who is prone to backache can experience particular problems. In recent years car manufacturers have paid much more attention to the design of the car seat and to the driving position in order to minimise backache. However, we still find seats that are poorly designed, holding the back in a rounded position. Sitting for a long time in this posture can cause excruciating back pain. The best car seats have a built-in adjustable lumbar support, and the height, seat and back angles can be altered to suit the individual driver. The foot controls should be squarely in front of your feet and not at an angle, as this causes constant spine twisting. Adequate wing mirrors will help you avoid having to twist round, and power steering will lessen the strain on your spine when manoeuvring at low speeds.

SITTING INCORRECTLY
Avoid sitting on a stool with your back bent forwards. It will aggravate any backache and cause stiffness.

SITTING PROPERLY

Many chairs are poorly designed. Often the worst are low armchairs and easy chairs that look temptingly soft but hold your back in a rounded position, causing severe aching and stiffness. Perching on a stool with your back bent forwards often aggravates backache and stiffness, so avoid it if you can. You will be most comfortable in an upright chair that supports your lower back, maintaining the normal slightly inward curve of the lumbar part of your spine.

If necessary, you can make your own lumbar support using a small cushion or a rolled-up towel, or put a back rest or lumbar roll behind the small of your back.

MONITORING MOVEMENTS

Bending forwards and twisting movements combined with carrying a heavy load are the most likely to stress your spine and produce back problems. Avoiding these types of stress is important for all of us, but especially for anyone with a back problem.

SITTING CORRECTLY
Try to sit upright with the natural curve of your back maintained and both feet flat on the floor.

39

LIFTING CORRECTLY

Many back problems develop during lifting. Frequently this arises when load bearing is combined with bending forwards and a twist on the spine. There are some simple practical guidelines that help to protect the back and reduce the risk of back trouble.

SAFE CARRYING
Never carry anything that is too heavy for you. Always keep the objects close to your body, and try to keep loads evenly balanced.

IS THE OBJECT TOO HEAVY?

The first priority when lifting is to decide whether the load is too heavy or bulky to move on your own. There are no hard and fast rules about the maximum weight that can be lifted safely. Much depends on the circumstances, the position that is required, the size, shape and weight of the object and on your personal physical strength and health.

The strain on your spine is much greater if the object is held at arm's length rather than close to your body. Someone with back problems can carry much less than a healthy adult. On the whole, men can carry heavier loads than women and young people.

Get a firm grip with the palms of your hands and the roots of your fingers and thumbs, rather than with your fingers alone. Heavy objects should not be lifted above shoulder level as this produces tremendous strain on the spine.

SLEEPING PROPERLY

A lot of people get backache from their bed. This is often because they have a poor quality mattress and base that sag under the weight of their body. Most of us sleep on our sides, so sagging produces

How to Lift Objects from the Floor

Lifting incorrectly is the root of many back problems. Follow the instructions below to minimise the risk of straining the ligaments in the back, which causes acute back pain.

STEP 1

The right way to lift is to place your feet apart, at right angles to each other, and with the front foot pointing in the direction to which the object is to be moved. This puts you in a stable position and prevents you from twisting your back in the process of lifting and then moving off.

STEP 2

Crouch down, bending your hips and knees but keeping your back straight. Your whole spine may be inclined forwards, but it is important to avoid bending your back. In this position, your knees are well apart and the object is positioned between them and kept close to your body. You can get a good, firm grip and the lift is performed using your leg muscles.

STEP 3

Once you are upright, you should carry the load close to your body without twisting your back. Put it down carefully, using the same procedure in reverse.
This is known as the kinetic method of lifting. Many industries train their workers to use this technique automatically, but it should be the lifting method used by everybody.

a sideways bend in the back that may lead to considerable aching and stiffness. You can largely stop this happening by sleeping on a bed that does not sag so easily. The ideal bed is one with a firm, well-sprung mattress and base, although it does not need to be hard.

In fact, it may be a mistake to buy a very firm, hard bed in the belief that it is good for your back, as it can be so uncomfortable that you don't sleep well. When you're choosing a bed, spend some time lying on it to ensure that it is firm but comfortable.

Unfortunately, a well-sprung, quality bed can be very expensive. An alternative, which is almost as effective, is to place a firm board on top of the base and underneath the mattress. It should run the full length of the bed and be thick enough not to bend under the weight of your body. A sheet of block board about three-quarters of an inch (2 cm) thick seems a very good choice for this purpose.

USING JUST ONE PILLOW

You should lie with your body as straight as possible so that neither your spine nor your neck bends sideways during the night. Too many pillows put a sideways twist on your neck that will be transmitted down your back. It is usually better to use only one pillow so that your head and neck are in line with the rest of your body when lying on your side.

STAYING IN SHAPE

If you are overweight, you are putting additional strain on your back, and you may also have a poor posture. Losing weight is important not only for your back, but also because it is good for your general health.

Physical fitness and exercise form an important part of prevention and treatment if you are prone to back problems. We strongly believe that exercise helps to prevent back pain by increasing the ability of the trunk to cope with loads.

There are many different types of suitable exercise, such as aerobics, weight-training and simple stretching and bending exercises (see pp.60–62). Keeping fit and strengthening your spine muscles is most important.

Unfortunately, some exercises can make back pain worse. If you have a back problem, it is important to take care and to concentrate on doing the kinds of exercise that are designed for strengthening the back and stomach muscles, rather than those aimed at forcing back movements.

KEEPING FIT
Your back will benefit from regular exercise and stretching, which helps to keep the spine muscles strong and flexible, and thereby prevents damage.

KEY POINTS

- Good posture is important for preventing backache.
- The shoes that we wear and the chairs that we sit on can also affect our backs: avoid high heels and sagging chairs.
- When lifting an object, follow the kinetic method of lifting, and avoid lifting very heavy objects.
- Make sure that your bed has a good, firm but comfortable mattress, and avoid using too many pillows.

What causes persistent back pain?

Some people suffer persistent or chronic back pain, and need careful investigation to find out why. Once the cause is identified, a proper treatment programme can be planned.

By far the most common cause of chronic back pain is some mechanical disorder in the back. However, in a small proportion of people, pain is the result of inflammatory diseases, disorders of bone, tumours or problems in the abdomen or pelvis.

MECHANICAL BACK PAIN

Many people suffer persistent pain in the back, which may spread into the buttock or the leg. Often, the pain is aggravated by physical activity and by certain postures. The spine is a very complicated structure and many different things can go wrong. The following are common causes of chronic mechanical back pain.

LUMBAR SPONDYLOSIS

X-rays of the back frequently show signs of ageing changes in the intervertebral discs and facet joints. Indeed they are present in almost every older person. Although people with these ageing changes more often get

AGGRAVATING FACTORS
A day's digging can exacerbate back pain from strained muscles and ligaments.

backache than those without, there is no clear cut correlation between wear and tear and the symptoms of back pain. A person may have quite severe X-ray evidence of wear and tear, and yet be symptom free. For this reason signs of wear and tear in the spine should be treated with caution. Just because you have them and also have backache does not mean that the changes are the cause of the symptoms. Nor does it mean that someone who has these changes but no backache is bound to develop back problems or become disabled in the future.

In lumbar spondylosis, the pain is felt across the lower back, and is sometimes worse on one side than the other. The pain worsens with physical exercise and bending, and is made easier by rest. However, some people tend to

EARLY MORNING STIFFNESS
People who have lumbar spondylosis often stiffen up after spending a long time in one position. This is especially common when rising from bed in the mornings.

stiffen when they stay in one position. This may be most noticeable first thing in the morning or after prolonged sitting in an easy chair. The pain can spread into one or other buttock and sometimes into the back of the thigh.

On examination, back movements are usually limited, but often this is only on certain types of movements, while other movements are relatively free.

PROLAPSED OR BURST DISC

Under stress the disc may burst – usually backwards and to one side – so that it presses on a nerve, leading to pain in the back that spreads down the leg. Commonly, the disc was already showing marked evidence of wear and tear damage and was seriously weakened. The particular stress precipitated the development of the burst that was about to occur. When the disc prolapses, the person may develop sciatica (see p.21). The problem may, unfortunately, persist and lead to long-term pain and disability.

The person suffering a prolapse will describe pain in the buttock usually spreading down the back or the outside of the thigh to the back of the calf and sometimes into the foot, usually the top or outer aspect. Frequently, the pain is accompanied by a sensation of tingling or pins and needles, which are known technically as paraesthesiae. This can be extremely painful and there may also be the sensation of numbness.

The examination reveals evidence that the nerve is trapped. When the leg is kept straight and lifted

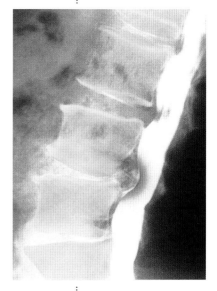

PAINFUL PRESSURE
In this false colour X-ray image, an intervertebral disc has burst backwards, pressing on the spinal cord (shown as white) at the point highlighted in pink.

47

upwards there is a lot of pain, and the movement is limited. There may be weakness of certain movements of the foot, and the ankle reflex can be lost. There may also be a reduction in the ability to feel in the area of the damaged nerve.

FLEXIBLE JOINTS
Hypermobility may predispose a person to joint problems in later life due to excessive wear and tear and overstretched ligaments.

HYPERMOBILITY

Some people have remarkably flexible joints. They can bend forwards with the legs straight to place the palms of their hands flat on the ground. The joints of the arms and legs can bend to a remarkable degree. This is known as hypermobility. Many sportsmen and sportswomen, trapeze artistes and professional dancers are hypermobile – it is this facility that enables them to undertake physical activities far beyond most of us.

Paradoxically, in later years hypermobility predisposes the individual to the development of joint symptoms. It is likely that repeated excessive movements have led to the development of wear and tear changes and to the over-stretching of ligaments. In particular, it is an important cause of back problems. It is remarkable how well back movements are preserved in these patients and sometimes they have difficulty in convincing their doctors that there is anything wrong, because their movements appear to be so good.

INHERITED VARIATIONS IN THE SPINE

We are all different shapes and sizes, and our spines vary accordingly. Some people are born with an extra lumbar vertebra or one too few, or with abnormally shaped vertebrae. These variations are usually unimportant and do not cause their owners any pain.

SPONDYLOLISTHESIS

Sometimes one vertebra slips forwards on top of the one below because of a weakness in the supporting arches of the vertebral column. This is called a 'spondylolisthesis' and can cause pain because it results in overstretching of nerves or ligaments.

This slipping may be the result of failure of the supporting bones in the back of the spine to develop properly or it may be due to wear and tear of the vertebrae themselves.

SPINAL STENOSIS

The nerve roots run down from the spinal cord within the column of vertebrae in the vertebral column and then emerge from the sides of the vertebral column through narrow openings (each known as a foramen, several as foramina). They then run down into the legs.

We all have spinal canals and foramina of different sizes and shapes. Some are smaller than others, putting the nerves that run through them at particular risk of getting squashed.

When this affects the central canal of the vertebral column it is known as central stenosis, and this may lead to pain, numbness and tingling in the legs, which develop on walking and are relieved by rest. These symptoms are quite similar to the leg problems associated with a poor blood supply to the legs. The pain is also made worse by arching backwards and relieved by bending forwards.

When the narrowing affects the foramina through which the nerve roots emerge, patients may develop persistent unremitting sciatica-type pain. This is known as foraminal stenosis. Surgery to relieve this type of nerve pressure can be very effective.

A PAINFUL NECK
Back pain that spreads into the neck area is one of the most common symptoms of fibromyalgia.

FIBROMYALGIA

People with fibromyalgia develop a range of symptoms. They experience widespread pain across the back spreading up the back of the chest into the neck and into the limbs. They often have tender points, particularly over the sacroiliac joints, the shoulder blades, the inside and outside of the elbows and knees, and elsewhere. Frequently, they have had a variety of detailed tests, but no particular abnormality can be pinpointed.

Many people with fibromyalgia are very upset and depressed; they feel tired and lacking in energy. It is often difficult for doctors to decide whether the persistent pain has led to the depression or whether the depression has led them to feel pain more severely. It may well be that the explanation lies in changes in the way pain sensations are transmitted in the spinal cord.

Many people with this condition sleep poorly and wake up in the mornings feeling unrefreshed, with generalised aches and pains and stiffness. Some research suggests that this poor sleep rhythm may actually be responsible for the problem. People with fibromyalgia often have other problems, such as irritable bowel syndrome and migraine.

OTHER CAUSES OF BACK PAIN

Although most backache is the result of mechanical disorders such as those I have described, in a small proportion of people it is a symptom of some other illness. For this reason you should always be thoroughly assessed by a doctor, particularly when back pain develops for the first time or when its nature suddenly changes. Other causes of back pain include the following.

INFECTION

Fortunately this is uncommon, but occasionally people with severe back problems are found to have chronic infection in the discs or elsewhere.

ANKYLOSING SPONDYLITIS

This is an inflammatory form of arthritis in which the effects are concentrated on the back. Sometimes it can attack the joints of the arms and legs, and occasionally other body tissues. Most often it starts in young adults, usually men. However, women sometimes get it and it can start at any age. The initial problems appear in the joints between the sacrum and the pelvis (sacroiliac joints) and may then spread up the spine. As it advances it can cause stiffening of the back and a pronounced stoop, and in severe cases the spine may end up completely rigid.

Unlike people who have mechanical backache, those with ankylosing spondylitis may find that their pain and stiffness are aggravated by rest and relieved by exercise. They often toss and turn in bed and wake up in the morning with aching and stiffness. Many get up in the night and do some physical exercise in order to obtain relief. As the condition worsens, the aching and stiffness may last longer through the day. Your doctor will examine you and probably organise blood tests and X-rays to confirm the diagnosis.

BONE DISORDERS

The skeleton provides the scaffolding that supports the soft tissues of the body. Unlike a metal framework, bone is a living material in which the constituents are constantly being renewed. There are several types of disease that lead to weakening and deformity of the bone and may make you more prone to fractures:

The Effects of Osteoporosis

Thinning of the interior of the bones makes them lighter, more fragile, brittle and much more prone to fracture. When the bones of the spine are affected, the weakened vertebrae may become crushed, causing pain and loss of height.

Strong, calcium-rich bone

Spaces between bony material are filled with marrow in living bone

NORMAL BONE TISSUE IN A VERTEBRA

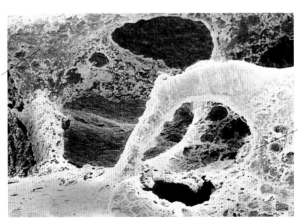

Bone mass lost as osteoblasts become inactive

Fragile, brittle bone material

OSTEOPOROTIC BONE TISSUE IN A VERTEBRA

● **Osteoporosis** This is a common form of bone disease. Most often it affects women after the menopause, when hormonal changes lead to weakening of bone structure, although men can and do get it, too. Some people develop osteoporosis as a result of hormonal disorders such as Cushing's disease or as a complication of treatment with certain steroid drugs.

When the bone is weakened, tiny fractures occur very easily and the vertebrae become squashed. Some people experience repeated attacks of severe back pain as a result and gradually develop a stoop.

The loss of height and severe bending forwards that can often affect older women is usually caused by osteoporosis.

● **Osteomalacia** People with this condition lack calcium and vitamin D. This can be the result of a poor diet low in dairy products, failure to absorb calcium from the bowel or lack of sunlight. Their bones become weaker, so that they are more prone to fractures and pain.

● **Paget's disease** This condition causes the bone to suddenly start growing very quickly, and it affects elderly people. The new bone is abnormal and soft and may fracture easily or press on nerves and ligaments causing tenderness and pain.

TUMOURS

Occasionally back pain may be caused by a tumour developing in the back or spreading from elsewhere. Although it is a rare cause of backache, the possibility has to be ruled out, which is why it is important to have a proper medical assessment.

REFERRED PAIN

This is the term doctors use to describe pain that you feel in your back but which actually has its origin somewhere else in your body.

Not all back pain is caused by problems in and around the spine – for example, it might be caused by disorders in the abdomen or pelvis. Stomach ulcers, gynaecological problems and some other conditions can result in pressure on nerves and cause back pain. When there is some link between bouts of pain and a woman's periods, doctors will consider whether there may be a gynaecological cause. Sometimes it is not obvious that the problem is actually arising in the abdomen or pelvis.

KEY POINTS

- There are a number of medical conditions that cause back pain, including many mechanical disorders.
- Back pain can also be a symptom of an illness such as inflammation, infection, bone disorders and referred pain.
- Changes associated with the ageing process can cause back problems in elderly people.
- In women after the menopause, osteoporosis can cause back pain and bending of the spine.

Treating persistent back pain

Treatment for persistent back pain may include a special exercise programme, drug therapy or, rarely, surgery. It is important to get your doctor's assessment of the problem before deciding on the appropriate treatment.

GETTING A DIAGNOSIS

A diagnosis can generally be made by clinical examination alone, but further tests may be necessary in some cases.

YOUR MEDICAL HISTORY

For your doctor, the most important part of assessing your back problem is finding out from you exactly how the pain started and what has happened since, together with other medical features. You will then have a physical examination. That may well be all that is necessary.

BLOOD TESTS

As we have already seen, most backaches have a mechanical cause, so the results of blood tests are normal. However, such

CLINICAL EXAMINATION
Your doctor will carry out a thorough physical examination, including a straight-leg raise, in order to make a diagnosis of back pain.

tests are useful when investigating possible inflammatory and other causes of back pain. In particular, ankylosing spondylitis (see p.51) is associated with a certain white blood cell type known as HLA-B27. If this is not present when your blood test results come back, you are very unlikely to have this condition. A blood test result that shows the presence of HLA-B27, however, does not prove that you do have ankylosing spondylitis, as this white cell type is found in about 8 per cent of healthy people who do not have this condition.

X-RAYS

Vast numbers of spine X-rays are taken but the majority are unnecessary. The only people who really need them are those with severe back pain that has failed to get better with simple treatment and those with complicated problems. Unnecessary X-rays should be avoided as each involves some, albeit slight, exposure to radiation.

RADICULOGRAPHY

When we look at X-rays of the spine we are actually studying shadows of the bones. This means we cannot see the soft tissues, such as the nerves and discs within the spine.

In a radiculogram (myelogram), dye that is opaque to X-rays is injected into the spinal column. When a disc has burst, the column of dye will be indented where the disc presses into the spinal column, so the exact location of the damaged disc can be identified on the X-ray.

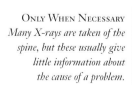

ONLY WHEN NECESSARY
Many X-rays are taken of the spine, but these usually give little information about the cause of a problem.

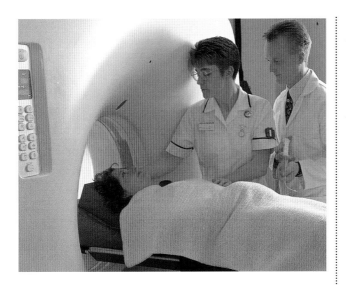

CT SCANNING
A patient enters a computed tomography scanner, which will give a detailed picture of the structures in the spine and may help to explain this person's symptoms.

CT SCANNING

CT stands for computed tomography. CT scans enable doctors to use X-rays to obtain a clearer view of the internal structures of the vertebral column. In particular, the inner outlines of the bony structures can be examined and some details of the discs can be seen.

MAGNETIC RESONANCE IMAGING

MRI involves the use of very strong magnetic fields rather than X-rays, and is particularly good for studying the nerves, ligaments and discs within the bony structures.

LIMITATIONS OF CT AND MRI

These imaging methods are gradually becoming more widely available. However, it's not always clear who can really benefit from being scanned in these ways. As with X-rays of the back, the changes that they reveal often correlate poorly with symptoms.

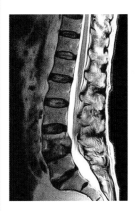

MRI SCANNING
As this MRI scan of the spine shows, the technique produces a high-quality image of the vertebrae, discs and surrounding muscles.

57

NON-DRUG TREATMENTS

How chronic back pain is treated depends on whether it is caused by mechanical problems – the most common kind – or by some other disorder.

LONG-TERM DISCOMFORT
Back problems frequently affect people who are overweight. Losing weight and taking up a carefully tailored programme will help to restore normal mobility.

CARING FOR YOUR BACK

Physical activity is good for people with chronic back problems. You should try to keep active and to exercise, although you do need to take some sensible precautions. You have to be careful, for example, to avoid over-stressing your back and to be aware of your posture when standing, sitting and lifting. Lifting heavy loads is not a job for you.

PHYSIOTHERAPY

Views on treatment have changed dramatically in the last few years. We now believe the principal role of the physiotherapist is to get you mobile again and restore you to normal levels of activity as soon as possible. It is important that you be referred to a physiotherapist if your back problem has lasted more than a few weeks and is in danger of becoming chronic.

The physiotherapist will teach you how your back works, what can go wrong, how to protect the back against excessive stresses and teach you exercises aimed at restoring your mobility so you can start to function normally again.

The exercise programme will normally be tailored to your individual needs, but will include ones to strengthen your back and abdominal muscles, together with pelvic tilt exercises.

Sometimes the physiotherapist will apply various forms of heat, such as an infrared lamp or short-wave diathermy; other aids include ice packs or cooling aerosol sprays, ultrasound or massage. Such treatments do not cure the long-term problem but can be extremely soothing and relaxing. Their special value is often as a preliminary to other forms of treatment such as exercises, which otherwise would be very painful.

Traction, like many of the treatments for back pain, has been used since ancient times. As you lie on a special traction table with one harness around your lower chest and another round your pelvis, the two halves of your body are gently pulled apart. The idea is to stretch damaged joints and relieve pressure on damaged nerves. It helps at the time, but its long-term value is doubtful and its use is becoming restricted. It is not worth rushing out to buy any of the expensive gadgets available on the market for home traction.

AT THE PHYSIOTHERAPIST
An examination that involves raising the leg stretches the sciatic nerve.

EXERCISES

There are many different types of exercise for people with chronic back pain, and the choice depends very much on the nature of your particular problem.

Some exercises may help one type of backache but make another worse, so be careful when planning your own exercise programme. You should discuss these first with your physiotherapist. The various types of exercise include those already described, aimed at strengthening

Exercises for Chronic Back Pain

A simple and safe programme of exercises should be undertaken in a graded and gradually increasing fashion. Initially do the following exercises once or twice, then gradually increase up to six times each day as your back allows. For many people, other types of exercise are required, but these should be performed only under the guidance of a physiotherapist because certain exercises can make some types of back pain worse. Much depends on the particular problems in each individual case.

EXERCISE 1   Lie flat on your back on the floor. Keep your legs straight and lift each heel in turn, just off the floor. Repeat.

EXERCISE 2   Lie flat on your back on the floor with a pillow under your head. Fold your arms. Lift your head and shoulders just off the floor and then lie flat and relax. Repeat.

EXERCISE 3   Lie flat on your back on the floor. Tense your stomach muscles and flatten the small of your back onto the floor, then relax. Repeat.

Exercises for Chronic Back Pain (cont'd.)

EXERCISE 4   Lie flat on your back. Reach down the side of one thigh towards your knee. Straighten up and repeat to the other side. Repeat.

Seen from above.

EXERCISE 5   STEP 1 Lie flat on your back on the floor. Bend your knees so that your feet are flat on the ground.

STEP 2 Lift your bottom in the air by tightening your stomach muscles, keeping the back straight. Repeat.

Exercises for Chronic Back Pain (cont'd.)

EXERCISE 6   Lie on your stomach on the floor, then do press-ups with your hands, but keeping your back straight. Repeat.

EXERCISE 7   **STEP 1** Kneel on all fours. Arch your back upwards.   **STEP 2** Now hollow your back. Flatten your back and repeat.

EXERCISE 8   **STEP 1**   **STEP 2**

STEP 1 Stand with your back against the wall, with your back forming its normal hollow.

STEP 2 Tighten your tummy muscles so that your back flattens against the wall. Then restore the normal hollow and repeat.

the back and abdominal muscles (known as isometric exercises), and those that improve movements of the back. It is important to avoid any exercises that make the pain suddenly worse. It is better to undertake a specific amount of exercise that is gradually increased each day.

SPORT

Sportsmen should keep active and return to sport as soon as possible after a bout of severe pain. The safest options are walking, swimming and cycling. Contact sports such as rugby are risky, as sudden, unexpected and forceful movements of the back can undo several weeks of gradual improvement.

RETURNING TO SPORT
People who are used to regular exercise should return to sport as soon as possible once their back pain has subsided. Swimming is one of the best and safest forms of exercise for back problems.

MOBILISATION AND MANIPULATION

If back pain is caused by mechanical displacement of one of the joints or discs then it should be possible to put things right by manipulation of the spine. This is the theory underlying the various techniques of mobilisation and manipulation. There is wide variety in the techniques practised by physiotherapists, osteopaths, chiropractors, physicians and orthopaedic surgeons.

Some manipulators apply forces directly to the vertebrae in the spine, whereas others use the shoulders and pelvis as levers.

There is no agreement by the various practitioners on the problems for which manipulation is useful, when the different types of manipulation should be used and the relative usefulness of these treatments.

Manipulation can hasten your recovery from an acute episode of back pain, but it is doubtful whether it provides real benefit for chronic back pain.

In general, manipulation appears to be safe, although a few people find that it makes their back problems worse. There is a very small risk of nerve damage when manipulation is performed under anaesthetic.

DRUG TREATMENTS

The main purpose of drug treatment is to relieve pain. The two main types of drugs used are pure pain relievers, known as analgesics, and those that also control inflammation in the area of damage, which are known as anti-inflammatory drugs. The character of the back problem is often helpful in indicating which type of drug will provide the most effective treatment.

PAINKILLERS

Paracetamol is the most commonly used painkiller. You can take up to six or eight 500 milligram tablets a day and it is very safe provided you don't exceed this dose. You can buy paracetamol by itself or combined with other drugs, such as codeine, from chemists without a doctor's prescription. There are several stronger analgesics, such as dextropropoxyphene and dihydrocodeine, which are often combined with paracetamol, but these are only available on prescription.

ANTI-INFLAMMATORY DRUGS

You will find these particularly helpful if you have a lot of stiffness in bed and when you wake up in the morning. Their main role is to reduce inflammation, but they are effective painkillers as well. Aspirin was the first anti-inflammatory drug, but it can cause indigestion and abdominal upsets, and larger doses may give you ringing noises in your ears and interfere with your hearing. Ibuprofen is available over the counter in pharmacies and seems to produce far fewer problems.

There are alternative anti-inflammatory drugs available on prescription, such as naproxen, diclofenac, piroxicam, ketoprofen and many others, generally taken in tablet form. A lot of research has gone into producing newer versions that need only be taken once or twice a day rather than every few hours – an obvious advantage.

All the anti-inflammatory drugs can cause abdominal upsets, so you may be prescribed an anti-ulcer treatment to take at the same time. Some of the newer anti-inflmamatory drugs, such as meloxicam, have a lower risk of stomach problems. Alternatively, if the anti-inflammatory tablets upset your system too much, your doctor can prescribe the drug in suppository form.

MUSCLE RELAXANTS

If you are one of those people who develop quite severe spasm of the back muscles, which can be very painful, you may find that muscle relaxant tablets are a help.

ANTI-EPILEPTIC DRUGS

Neuralgic pains are sudden electric shock sensations shooting from the back down the leg, often accompanied by painful tingling and numbness. These seem to result from over-sensitivity of the damaged nerves. People with epilepsy have over-sensitive brain cells, which fire off in an uncontrolled way, causing them to have seizures (or fits). The same drugs that are used to counter that problem can also be effective in relieving neuralgic pain.

TRICYCLIC ANTIDEPRESSANTS

Some people who have chronic back problems develop widespread pain and often their skin becomes hypersensitive so that it is tender to even light pressure. Alteration in the pain-processing system in the central nervous system probably underlies this. This type of pain is not helped by conventional pain-relieving tablets. There may be similar biochemical changes in the central nervous systems of people who are clinically depressed, and the drugs used for treating depression, such as amitriptyline, can be effective for treating this kind of pain.

INJECTIONS

Injections can be very helpful for certain types of back pain. They take a number of different forms depending on the precise nature of the problem.

- **For tender spots** Some people with back problems have one or two very localised tender areas in their back – perhaps in the superficial tissues, in the ligaments connecting the vertebrae, the sacroiliac joints or elsewhere. Your doctor can identify the painful areas by feeling your back carefully while you are lying flat in a relaxed position. The tender spots may then be treated with an injection of a small amount of local anaesthetic and a powerful steroid, such as cortisone. Steroids also have long-lasting anti-inflammatory action. After the injection you will usually be pain free for 2–3 hours due to the anaesthetic, then the pain may return for 24 hours or so. However, after that period, some people find that their pain diminishes dramatically. How long this relief lasts varies considerably from one person to another, but for many it is long lasting. Cortisone used in this way does not cause the adverse effects that may develop when it is taken regularly by mouth.

● **Facet joint injections** Sometimes the problem arises in the facet joints at the back of the spine, and this can also be treated by means of an injection using a fine needle. It is usually done under X-ray guidance so that the injection can be positioned in precisely the right place in the joint.

● **Epidural injections** An epidural injection is given into the spine around the linings surrounding the spinal cord and nerve roots. Local anaesthetic with a small amount of a cortisone-like drug is injected. You may be offered this if you have sciatica that has improved after a severe attack but has not cleared up completely.

COMPLEMENTARY TREATMENTS

Some people find that their back pain responds well to complementary treatments such as acupuncture.

ACUPUNCTURE

Back pain can be very difficult to control. Sometimes, the symptoms are relieved by blocking the passage of nerve impulses up the spine to the brain.

Acupuncture was first developed in China between 2,000 and 3,000 years ago. It was thought to work by altering the balance between the two opposing life forces known as Yin and Yang. Acupuncture is often used in Western medicine today. We now know that it stimulates the release of natural chemicals known as endorphins and enkephalins within the brain and spinal cord, which can block the passage of the pain sensations. Sterile needles are inserted through the skin and then rotated to produce

ACUPUNCTURE NEEDLES
A method of pain relief that involves inserting fine needles into particular points on the body, acupuncture may be used as a complementary treatment for back pain.

stimulation. Some acupuncturists use the traditional Chinese acupuncture sites, but for many this is out of custom rather than belief.

Acupuncture does not work on everybody. Some people respond well, others derive only short-term benefit and need repeated treatment, and some people find that acupuncture makes no difference at all.

TENS TREATMENT

The problem with acupuncture is that inserting needles through the skin and applying stimulation is a highly skilled technique, and you will have to attend a special clinic to have it done. TENS (which stands for transcutaneous electrical nerve stimulation), on the other hand, is a treatment that you can give yourself in your own home.

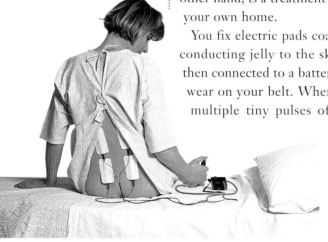

Using a TENS Machine
The electrical pads of a TENS machine are applied directly to the back. Your doctor may show you how to use this equipment in hospital, but it is easy to apply at home.

You fix electric pads coated with a special electrical conducting jelly to the skin of your back. These are then connected to a battery and stimulator, which you wear on your belt. When you switch the gadget on, multiple tiny pulses of electricity stimulate your skin, and you can adjust the strength, frequency and length of time of each impulse to suit yourself.

The electrical stimulation feels like a tiny pricking sensation in your skin. It acts in a similar way to acupuncture by stimulating nerves, and it releases substances in the brain and spinal cord that block the sensation of back pain.

This technique is useful for someone with chronic back pain who can switch on the stimulator whenever he or she needs it. As with acupuncture, TENS does not help everyone, but if you have persistent pain you should discuss with your doctor the possibility of using TENS. The treatment can sometimes be remarkably successful.

CORSETS

The lumbar support or corset consists of a firm body belt stretching from the rib cage to the pelvis with strengtheners behind, which may be flat steel strips moulded to the shape of the back.

Wearing a lumbar support limits your back movements and increases the pressure within your abdomen and therefore may relieve back pain.

Unfortunately, wearing a corset for a long time can lead to permanent back stiffness and in the long run many corsets do as much harm as good.

We now believe that, for most people, the aim should be to restore movements to the back as soon as possible, which is why corsets are now used only rarely.

SURGICAL TREATMENTS

It is estimated that only about one operation is needed for every 2,000 attacks of back pain. Surgery should only be considered if your symptoms have not responded to other treatment, if you have severe and persisting pain, and if your problem is of the type likely to improve after an operation. This means that surgery is unlikely to be considered as soon as an attack of back pain develops. Rather, other types of treatment will be tried first, and most people recover without the need for an operation. If you reach the point where an operation is being considered, your surgeon will arrange for detailed investigations to be performed.

Only certain types of back problems are likely to respond well to surgery. In particular there are very good results for those who have severe sciatic pain in the leg. About 80 to 90 per cent of people are very pleased with the results. On the other hand, the success rate is not nearly as good for those whose main problem is pain in the back itself.

WHAT OPERATION?

There are several different types of back operation. The most common is to remove a prolapsed disc – this is most commonly the disc between the fourth and fifth lumbar vertebrae, or between the fifth lumbar vertebra and the sacrum. In order to prevent any recurrence, the whole disc is usually removed and not just the burst area. In some cases the main problem is caused by pressure on the nerve roots from the bone of the vertebral column. The surgeon will aim to relieve this by taking away bone to create more space. Sometimes there is excessive movement between the bones of the vertebral column, in which case the surgeon may decide to fix the vertebrae together. This is known as a spinal fusion.

CONVALESCENCE

After surgery you will probably start to get up and walk within a few days. Often you have to wear a lumbar support for a few weeks but you may well get back to light work within a month or two. It will be several months before you can consider doing any heavy manual work. You should always ask your surgeon before undertaking any activities that are likely to cause excessive loads on your spine.

INTENSIVE REHABILITATION

A small proportion of people with chronic back pain develop very severe symptoms and unfortunately become extremely disabled.

There are a number of reasons for this, including not only the mechanical forms of damage around the spine, but also scarring that may develop around the nerve roots. There may be other changes that can occur within the central nervous system itself, and the whole problem is often exacerbated by depression and anxiety.

Unfortunately, this type of back pain can be very difficult to treat. People in this situation will often need a careful and sympathetic professional assessment of the problem. This will include not only an analysis of the physical problem but also of the patient's reactions to it. The next stage is then to design an intensive rehabilitation programme tailored to the requirements of the particular individual. This programme aims not only to restore physical function but also to help the person concerned to cope with the problem and to lead a more normal life.

This type of treatment can be very effective for the most severely disabled back sufferers. Unfortunately the availability of this type of programme, such as the one that we run in the Manchester and Salford Back Pain Centre, is extremely limited and is currently provided at very few centres in Britain.

It is hoped that these facilities will become more widely available before too long.

GETTING SPECIALIZED HELP
People with a severely disabling back problem often benefit from an individually tailored rehabilitation programme that is designed to restore both mobility and confidence.

71

KEY POINTS

- The history and clinical examination are the most important parts of assessment. Imaging tests are a useful supplement in appropriate cases.

- The back sufferer should understand how the back works, what goes wrong and why various types of treatment are used.

- Exercise is good for the back, but sudden, forceful movements should be avoided.

- The choice of tablets is related to the clinical problem. Most patients will be controlled by a simple painkiller, such as paracetamol, or anti-inflammatory drugs, such as ibuprofen.

- Surgery is only rarely necessary. On the whole it works a lot better for sciatic pain in the leg than for back pain alone.

- Intensive rehabilitation programmes are effective for people with severe chronic back problems.

Useful addresses

There are several national societies that are concerned with the welfare of people with back pain and with raising funds for research for better methods of diagnosis and treatment. Several of these organisations produce helpful booklets that provide useful factual information.

The Arthritis Research Campaign

Copeman House
St. Mary's Court,
St. Mary's Gate
Chesterfield
Derbyshire S41 7TD
Tel: (01246) 558033

This charity finances an extensive programme of research and education in a wide range of arthritis and rheumatism problems including back pain. It provides useful booklets that explain the various back problems and ways of coping with them.

Arthritis Care

18 Stephenson Way
London NW1 2HD
Tel: (0171) 916 1500

This charity provides information and advice for those who are disabled by all forms of arthritis and back pain. In particular, it runs holiday hotels for people disabled with arthritis and publishes a quarterly newsletter, *Arthritis News*, which is sent to all members.

National Ankylosing Spondylitis Society

Po Box 179
Mayfield
East Sussex TN20 6ZL
Tel: (01435) 873 527

This charity is for patients with ankylosing spondylitis, their families and friends, and doctors and research workers concerned with this problem. It provides practical advice and help, and holds open meetings for members. It publishes a useful handbook, a cassette tape of physiotherapy exercises, a twice-yearly journal and other publications.

National Back Pain Association
16 Elmtree Road
Teddington
Middlesex TW11 8ST
Tel: (0181) 977 5474
This charity has local branches
throughout the country with regular
meetings to disseminate information and
advice for people with back pain. Its
mission is to fund patient-orientated
scientific research into the causes and
treatment of back pain, to educate people
to use their bodies sensibly and so reduce
the incidence of back pain, and to form
and support branches through which
sufferers and those who care for them
may receive information, advice and
mutual help.

National Osteoporosis Society
PO Box 10,
Radstock
Bath BA3 3YB
Tel: (01761) 471771
This is a charitable organisation that
provides advice and support for people
with osteoporosis and seeks to improve
general awareness and to sponsor research
into this problem.

The Spinal Injuries Association
76 St James' Lane
London N10 3DF
Tel: (0181) 444 2121
This charity is for spinal cord injury
people, their families and friends. It
offers a range of services for paraplegics
and tetraplegics. It publishes a regular
newsletter with useful practical advice
and help.

Notes

Notes

Index

Acknowledgements

PUBLISHER'S ACKNOWLEDGEMENTS
Dorling Kindersley would like to thank the following for their help
and participation in this project:

Production Controller Michelle Thomas; **Consultancy** Dr. Sue Davidson;
Indexing Indexing Specialists, Hove; **Administration** Christopher Gordon.

Organisations St.John's Ambulance,
St.Andrew's Ambulance Organisation, British Red Cross.

Illustrations (p.12, p.13, p.14, p.20, p.22, p.23, p.27,
jacket: top left and bottom centre) © Philip Wilson.

Picture research Angela Anderson; **Picture librarian** Charlotte Oster.

PICTURE CREDITS
The publisher would like to thank the following for their kind
permission to reproduce their photographs. Every effort has been made
to trace the copyright holders. Dorling Kindersley apologises for any
unintentional omissions and would be pleased, in any such cases,
to add an acknowledgement in future editions.

APM Studios p.60, p.61, p.62; **Sally & Richard Greenhill Photo Library** p.9, p.63;
Institute of Orthopaedics p.57; **Science Photo Library** p.19 (Keene/BSIP),
p.30 (Sheila Terry), p.47 (BSIP, Ducloux), p.52 (Professor P. Motta),
p.57 (Jerome Yeats), p.58 (Tirot/BSIP), p.71 (John Greim).